SPECTRUM® READERS

LEVEL 3

MIGHTY Castles

D1507547

RIF Reading Is Fundamental

This book belongs to:

MARIA CAMILA & SAMUEL MARCEL V.M.

For more fun and activities, visit rif.org/kids.

PROUDLY SUPPORTED BY

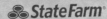
StateFarm®

SPECTRUM®

An imprint of Carson-Dellosa Publishing, LLC
P.O. Box 35665
Greensboro, NC 27425-5665

© 2014, Carson-Dellosa Publishing, LLC. Except as permitted under
the United States Copyright Act, no part of this publication may
be reproduced, stored, or distributed in any form or by any means
(mechanically, electronically, recording, etc.) without the prior written
consent of Carson-Dellosa Publishing, LLC. Spectrum is an imprint of
Carson-Dellosa Publishing, LLC.

carsondellosa.com

Printed in the USA. All rights reserved.
ISBN 978-1-4838-0130-8

01-002141120

Picture a castle.
What comes to mind?
Do you think of kings, queens,
and knights?
Do you imagine towers, moats, and
epic battles?
Read on to find out what medieval
(mee DEE vuhl) castles were
really like.
These castles were
built during the Middle
Ages, in AD 500–1500.
Many can still be visited
and explored today.

A Safe Home

Castles were homes for nobles—kings, queens, princes, dukes, lords, and barons. They were lively places that held royal feasts, jousting contests, and festivals with acrobats and storytellers.

Their most important role, however, was to protect the people inside from attacking armies.

Almost every part of a castle was built with protection in mind.

Fascinating Facts

- Castles were dark, damp, and very difficult to heat.

- A castle was a symbol of the owner's wealth and power. Castles were meant to look grand and fearsome.

Early Castles

The first castles were built from wood. Unfortunately, attackers could shoot burning arrows and set them on fire. Wood castles also tended to rot quickly. Stone castles were much stronger. Stone walls could be up to 20 feet thick! They offered protection against battering rams—wood and metal beams used by enemies to knock down walls.

Fascinating Facts

- A castle being attacked was said to be *under siege*.

- Early castles were built before guns and cannons were in use. Many of their defenses would not have stood up to a cannon's blast.

Castle Defense

A castle's stone walls were often built with narrow slits.

Archers could aim and shoot arrows through the slits, and they stayed protected behind the walls.

Castle towers were often built with gaps for the same reason.

A castle's thick stone walls provided the best protection during an attack.

Fascinating Facts

- A *garrison* was a group of soldiers who lived in a castle and defended it.

- Catapults let attackers hurl huge stones at a castle from a distance.

Moats

Moats often surrounded castles.
A moat was a large ditch full of water.
It kept attackers from coming right up to
a castle's walls and stopped the enemy
from tunneling under walls.
If water was scarce, moats were
left empty.
Because of their steep sides, they were still
very hard to cross!

Fascinating Facts

- A drawbridge was a movable bridge used to cross a moat. When it was up, no one could enter the castle.

- Some attackers brought portable bridges with them!

Towers

Early towers were shaped like squares.
Towers in this shape could be unstable.
Attackers could dig below the foundation.
Then, the tower would topple!
Builders found that round towers were
harder to knock down.
They were harder to build, too.
Because they offered more protection,
they became popular.

Fascinating Facts

- Towers could also be shaped like rectangles, polygons, or the letter D.
- In later castles, some towers held churches, kitchens, and latrines (or bathrooms).

Trim Castle

Trim Castle is the largest castle in Ireland. Owner Hugh de Lacy and his son built it over 30 years in the 1100s.

The castle has a three-story *keep*, or main tower, which has 20 sides!

Trim Castle was built on raised ground overlooking a river, giving guards a good view of the surrounding land.

They could see enemies coming from a great distance.

Fascinating Facts

- The movie *Braveheart* was filmed at Trim Castle.
- The keep was protected by a ditch, a stone wall, and a moat.

Cochem Castle

Cochem Castle looks like it belongs in a fairy tale.

It is more than 1,000 years old.

Like many other castles, it was built on a hill, over a river.

French troops set the castle on fire in 1689 and nearly destroyed it.

In 1868, a businessman bought the ruins and rebuilt the famous castle.

Today, it is owned by the city of Cochem, Germany.

Fascinating Facts

- In its early days, castle dwellers collected tolls from ships on the Mosel River below.

- Cochem Castle was owned by at least four different kings.

Harlech Castle

Harlech Castle stands on a cliff over the ocean in North Wales.

It is a concentric (con SEN trik) castle. Rings of stone walls were built inside one another, making a strong defense.

If attackers made it past one wall, they would run into another!

Fascinating Facts

- At one time, nearly 1,000 builders were working at Harlech Castle!

- Today, the castle is a World Heritage Site—a protected place that is important to a culture.

Carcassonne

Carcassonne is more than just a castle in France—it is an entire medieval city! It is a *fortified*, or protected, city. A double row of walls surrounds it, stretching almost two miles. The city also has 56 watchtowers! It took thousands of soldiers to guard it.

Fascinating Facts

- Fake stairs in Narbonne Tower were built to keep intruders away.

- In one tower room, there was space for hundreds of pigs and cattle. The meat could feed soldiers who could not leave during an attack.

21

Castelgrande

Castelgrande is one of three castles around the town of Bellinzona, Switzerland.

It stands on top of a rocky hill about 165 feet above the town.

Work on the castle started in the 1200s.

It has two towers, the White Tower (*Torre Bianca*) and the Black Tower (*Torre Nera*).

Fascinating Facts

- Castelgrande has been called *Old Castle*, *Un Castle*, and *Saint Michael's Castle*.

- More buildings were once part of the castle. They may have been destroyed in the 1400s.

23

Swallow's Nest Castle

Some buildings look like castles, but were not really built for protection.
Swallow's Nest Castle is one.
It was built in 1912—long after medieval times.
The structure, which resembles a sandcastle, stands on a cliff over the Black Sea in the Ukraine.
Today, you can visit a restaurant inside!

Fascinating Facts

- In 1927, an earthquake cracked the cliff below the castle. A huge concrete plate fixed it.

- Swallow's Nest Castle appears in several movies.

25

Japanese Castles

Not all castles are in Europe.
Many were built in Japan in the 1500s and 1600s.
Japanese castles often had many courtyards, or *baileys*.
The main tower sat at the center.
Some of these castles were built on wood bases.
Stone covered the wood to protect it from fire.

Fascinating Facts

- A Japanese samurai was similar to a knight. He was a warrior who served a lord or a king.
- The roofs of Japanese castles were curved and layered, like those on a pagoda.

27

Mont-Saint-Michel

Mont-Saint-Michel (mon san MEE shel) is a castle-like abbey on a French island. An *abbey* is a place where nuns and monks live and work.

Outer walls that protect the abbey were built after cannons came into use. Passageways between the walls allowed soldiers to travel around the building. During the French Revolution, the abbey was used as a prison.

Fascinating Facts

- In the 1800s, a *causeway*, or long bridge, was built to Mont-Saint-Michel.
- Just 13 nuns and monks remain at the abbey today.

Looking Back

The castles of the Middle Ages give us a peek into the past.

Their beautiful turrets, towers, and moats spark our imaginations.

Castles are relics from a dangerous time when many armies battled for land.

These fortresses no longer need to defend the people inside, but they do protect an important piece of history.

Fascinating Facts

- The great age of castles began almost 1,000 years ago and lasted for 500 years.

- The largest castle in England is Windsor Castle, one of the homes where the royal family lives today.

MIGHTY! Castles
Comprehension Questions

1. What was a castle's most important role?

2. When were the Middle Ages?

3. What was the purpose of the narrow slits in a castle's walls?

4. Where in a castle was a moat found?

5. Which tower shape was stronger, round or square?

6. Why were castles often built on hills?

7. Why do you think many castles were built overlooking a river?

8. Give two reasons why stone castles were better than wood castles.

9. In what way is Swallow's Nest Castle different from castles of the Middle Ages?

10. What is the largest castle in Ireland?

11. Where is Mont-Saint-Michel?

12. What protected the main tower in a Japanese castle?